A SEAPORT THROUGH HISTORY

This book takes us on a journey through the centuries. Lebek is an imaginary city and port based on a typical port on the North Sea and Baltic coasts of northern Europe. We trace its development from a tiny Bronze Age settlement beside an estuary around 3,000 years ago, to a great 20th-century city and port.

With the arrival of the Vikings in the 8th century, we follow the development of the settlement into a fortified seaport. We trace its rise as a great trading centre and follow the fortunes of its brave citizens, who, throughout the centuries and to this day, fight a continuing battle to keep out the sea from their reclaimed lands.

The book features fourteen large drawings of the developing seaport, each illustrating a different historical stage. Each drawing is followed by two pages of vivid narrative, and specific detailed illustrations keyed to the text.

INTRODUCTION

Lebek is an imaginary seaport in Northern Europe. Told through words and pictures, the story of our fictional city is based on research into the development of certain important European seaports along the North Sea and Baltic coasts.

Lebek could be in northern France, Belgium, The Netherlands, Denmark or northern Germany. The geographical, historical and cultural development of towns such as Antwerp, Rotterdam, Hamburg, Lubeck, Gdansk, have been taken as models for Lebek. These cities, although different in many ways, have historic, economic and cultural similarities. And they all have the sea, and sea trade, in common.

Lebek's origins are as obscure as those of the early peoples whose cultures developed along the coast of the North and Baltic Seas. These people evolved in isolation, scarcely influenced by the spreading Graeco-Roman culture. During the late Middle Ages, however, technical advances, and a growing knowledge of seafaring, brought civilization to the northern European coastal areas.

Lebek's situation, at the mouth of a wide river estuary, commanding busy sea routes and with excellent lines of communication inland, was ideal. These natural advantages, combined with the shrewd business sense of its citizens, brought about the city's development into a major centre for international trade.

1. THE MEGALITH BUILDERS (10th century BC to 1st century AD)

2. VIKING INVASIONS
(LATE 8TH CENTURY AD)

Over the centuries, the Leb estuary gradually changed. The deforestation and cultivation of inland areas increased the amount of silt carried down by the river, causing land to build up at the river mouth.

The Germanic peoples who lived near this northern coast hardly felt the impact of the civilization that was spreading throughout the

The settlers grew their precarious crops on the highest ground and Roman world. They maintained their old way of life, disturbed only by the occasional migrations of peoples from the west. Suddenly, in the early 8th century AD, the Leb estuary began to change. A recognizable town grew up on one of the little islands in the river. The townsfolk, however, did not come from the mainland but from across the seas.

For some years, fleets of Viking ships had been appearing in the estuary at intervals. These expert seafarers were on the lookout for trade and pillage. They also came to explore new lands, surveying the countryside in the hope of settling their growing population, which could no longer be fed in their barren northern homeland.

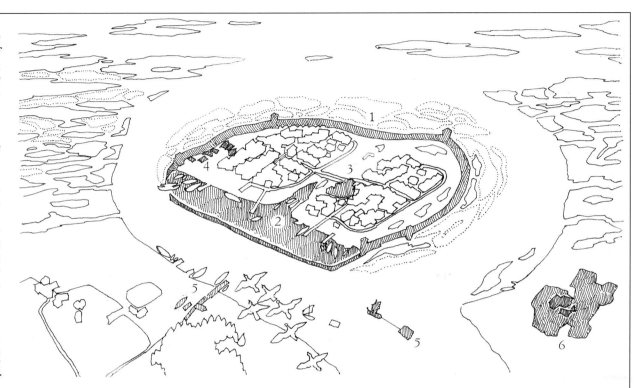

1. Walls
The town was defended against surprise attacks by walls made of mud and reeds strengthened with tree trunks. Barriers of stakes driven into the ground also protected the harbour.

2. The harbour
The harbour was situated on the sheltered side of the estuary, away from the wind and sea currents. For extra safety, the inhabitants could drag their lightweight boats up on to the sand. Sea-going vessels from the Baltic and North Seas would often get becalmed or run aground in the port. The goods that they carried were stored in the harbour's warehouses.

3. Houses
The town's merchants, craftsmen and seamen lived in simple houses made of reeds, mud and twigs. The roof was made of earth and grass. Some of the streets were paved with planks of wood, which helped people keep their feet out of the mud.

4. Foreign traders' camps
Visiting traders lived in flimsy huts and makeshift houses that could easily be put up and taken down again.

5. Dockyards
Under the Vikings, shipbuilding was already highly advanced. The different cuts and varieties of wood which were needed for building these ships were obtained from further inland and transported down the river.

6. Viking farming
The farmers grew crops and kept sheep and cattle. Outbuildings were grouped around the central home: these included granaries, stables and slave quarters.

A VIKING'S HOUSE
1. **Dry-stone walls and wooden uprights**
2. **Roof made of twigs, brushwood and turfs**
3. **Hearth**
4. **Loom**
5. **Bed**

Because it was sheltered from storms, the Leb estuary provided a safe haven for the Vikings. One of the little islands in the river was easy to defend and provided a secure refuge for this band of bold northern seafarers. From this island they could quickly reach the open sea and they could also explore the upper reaches of the river, sailing into the heart of the mainland. The Vikings, with their swift vessels — longships with terrifying dragons' heads — raised terror as they attacked the towns and villages they encountered on the way.

As time passed, the Viking encampment on the island in the Leb estuary grew into an established seaport, which they named Levfjord. Pillage was gradually replaced by trade, which brought more wealth and was less hazardous. Levfjord, ruled by the Viking nobility, became a prosperous trading port. Ships from northern seas and smaller river craft from inland, all came to dock at Levfjord, with the aim of trading with each other. Their cargoes consisted of salted fish, leather, footwear, woollen cloth, clay pots, bronze or iron cauldrons, amber beads, tools, weapons and slaves.

Levfjord prospered. Land around the estuary was reclaimed for the cultivation of crops. In the workshops, iron weapons were forged and exquisite woollen cloth was woven. Warring ceased, and the Vikings intermarried with the native inhabitants of the coast and became Christian. By the beginning of the 11th century, Levfjord, now more often known as Lebecburg, had become an independent town, although still under the rule of the feudal earldom of the lower Leb.

1. Hull
2. Planking
3. Cross timbers
4. Step for base of mast
5. Dragon's head prow being carved
6. Steering oar

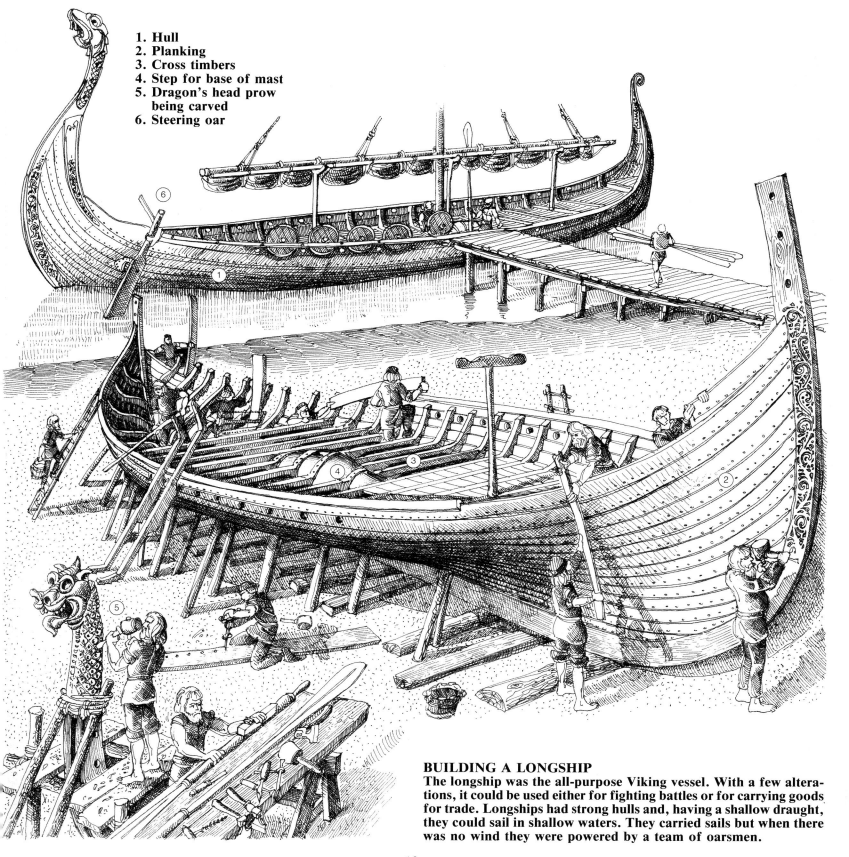

BUILDING A LONGSHIP

The longship was the all-purpose Viking vessel. With a few alterations, it could be used either for fighting battles or for carrying goods for trade. Longships had strong hulls and, having a shallow draught, they could sail in shallow waters. They carried sails but when there was no wind they were powered by a team of oarsmen.

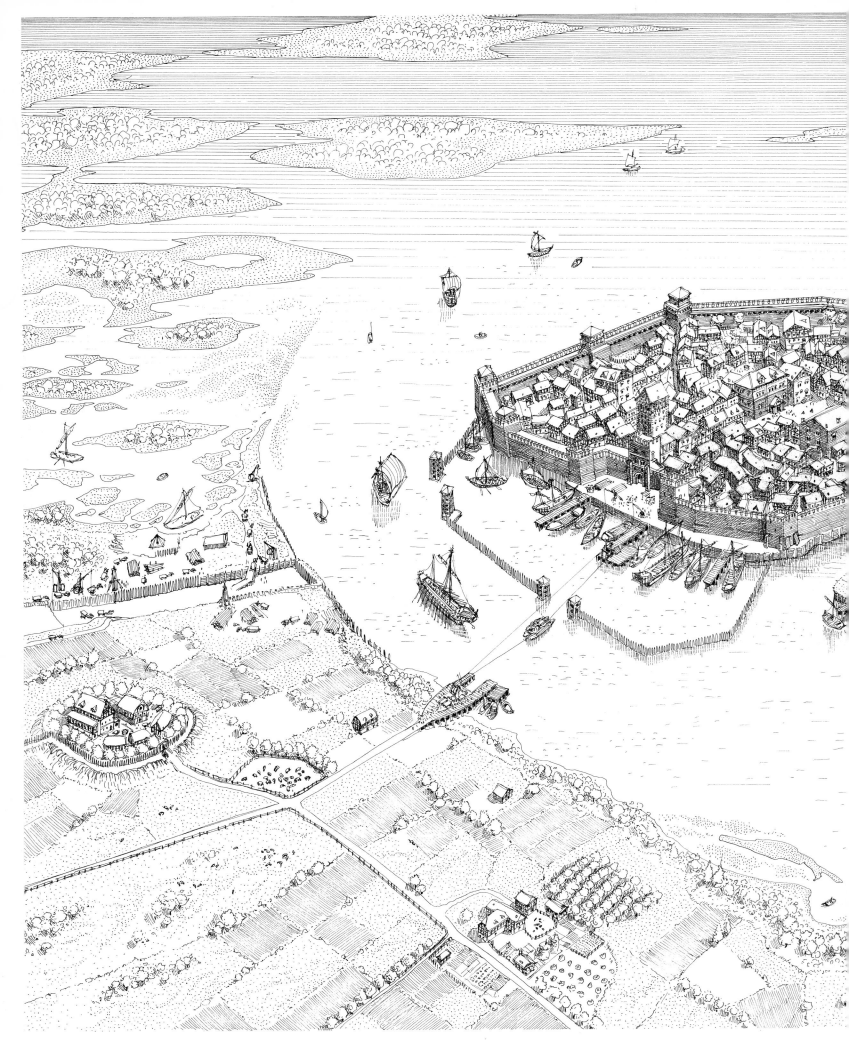

3. A FREE CITY IN FEUDAL EUROPE (early 13th century)

3. A FREE CITY IN FEUDAL EUROPE
(EARLY 13TH CENTURY)

At the end of the 12th century, trade developed further in the southern coastal areas of the North and Baltic Seas. The old ways of trading — by barter and exchange — died out as new ways of commerce were adopted. The old Scandinavian oared longships were replaced by a new kind of ship, the coggen, powered entirely by sail, that could carry up to 100 tonnes of goods. At the same time, merchants in the trading ports joined together to strengthen their position. Towns in the area were allied politically and some of them formed a league known as the Hanse, with which the merchants of Lebecburg were associated.

Lebecburg, now beginning to be called Lebek, made the most of the new network of trading centres around the North and Baltic Seas. By this time, the city was fully integrated with the mainland; its Viking origins were now only a memory. The Norse pirates who still occasionally sailed from Scandinavia, periodically appearing in the Leb estuary, were now regarded as dangerous barbarians.

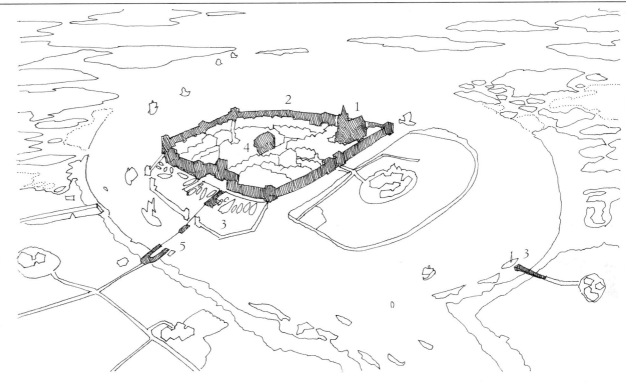

1. Romanesque cathedral
The cathedral was built in hewn stone in the style already used in France and Germany. It was strong and solid, contrasting sharply with the flimsy dwellings of the townspeople. The building of cathedrals and other such public places was usually financed by the craftsmens' and merchants' guilds.

2. Ramparts
The ramparts were initially made of stone, wood and cement. They protected the people against possible surprise attacks, either from sea or land. But the ramparts kept the city isolated from the dock area.

3. The docks
At the beginning of the 13th century, boats were still small and light enough to be dragged up on to the sand. Larger boats were moored alongside the wooden stockades and jetties.

4. The Diet
The Diet, the city's governing body, had its headquarters in a building in a prominent position in the centre of the city. Documents and other records were kept there. This building was also the city's administrative headquarters.

5. The ferry
There were no fixed bridges linking the city to the mainland, an advantage when it came to defence in times of uncertainty. Ferries plied back and forth from the city to the mainland on a cable stretched between the two banks.

HOW AN ORDINARY HOUSE WAS BUILT

1. **The frame and rafters, made of wood from nearby forests**
2. **The walls, built up from a framework of branches plastered with clay. In later times, bricks were used**
3. **The roof is covered with a thatch of twigs and straw**

Although Lebek was formally tied to the dukedom of Leb, the city was able to maintain a certain amount of independence and did not have to pay taxes or excise duty. The dukes of Leb gave the people of Lebek complete freedom. The prosperous farming community, which bought and sold its wares in Lebek, brought great wealth to the dukedom. Surplus crops from the fields, wool from the flocks of sheep and woollen cloth woven by the countrypeople, were brought to market in the town, and Lebek became a busy centre for the production and exchange of goods.

Although a small number of noblemen lived in Lebek, it was the powerful merchants who held power and organized the town. A council of these wealthy merchants, called the Diet, controlled all that went on. Safe within wide stone ramparts, Lebek was now protected against attack, both from the sea and from the mainland.

During the 11th century, a Romanesque cathedral was built from stone which had been hewn at quarries inland, and brought to the town by riverboat. The houses of craftsmen, merchants and the headquarters of the Diet were huddled together within the safety of the walls. One of the few open spaces in the city was the central square, where the guildhall stood.

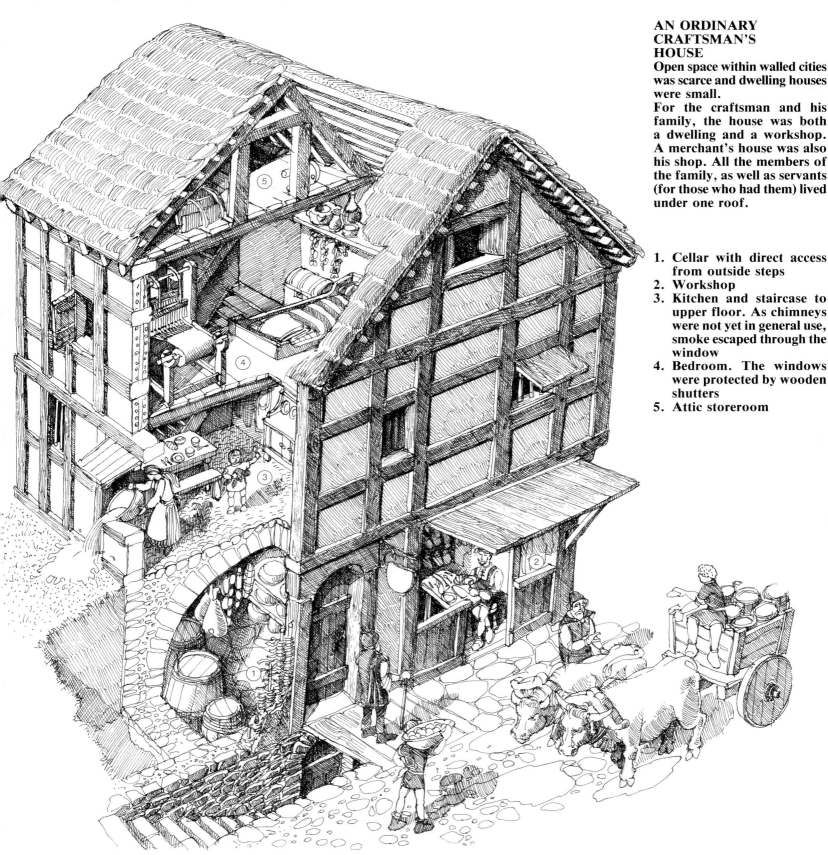

AN ORDINARY CRAFTSMAN'S HOUSE

Open space within walled cities was scarce and dwelling houses were small.

For the craftsman and his family, the house was both a dwelling and a workshop. A merchant's house was also his shop. All the members of the family, as well as servants (for those who had them) lived under one roof.

1. **Cellar with direct access from outside steps**
2. **Workshop**
3. **Kitchen and staircase to upper floor. As chimneys were not yet in general use, smoke escaped through the window**
4. **Bedroom. The windows were protected by wooden shutters**
5. **Attic storeroom**

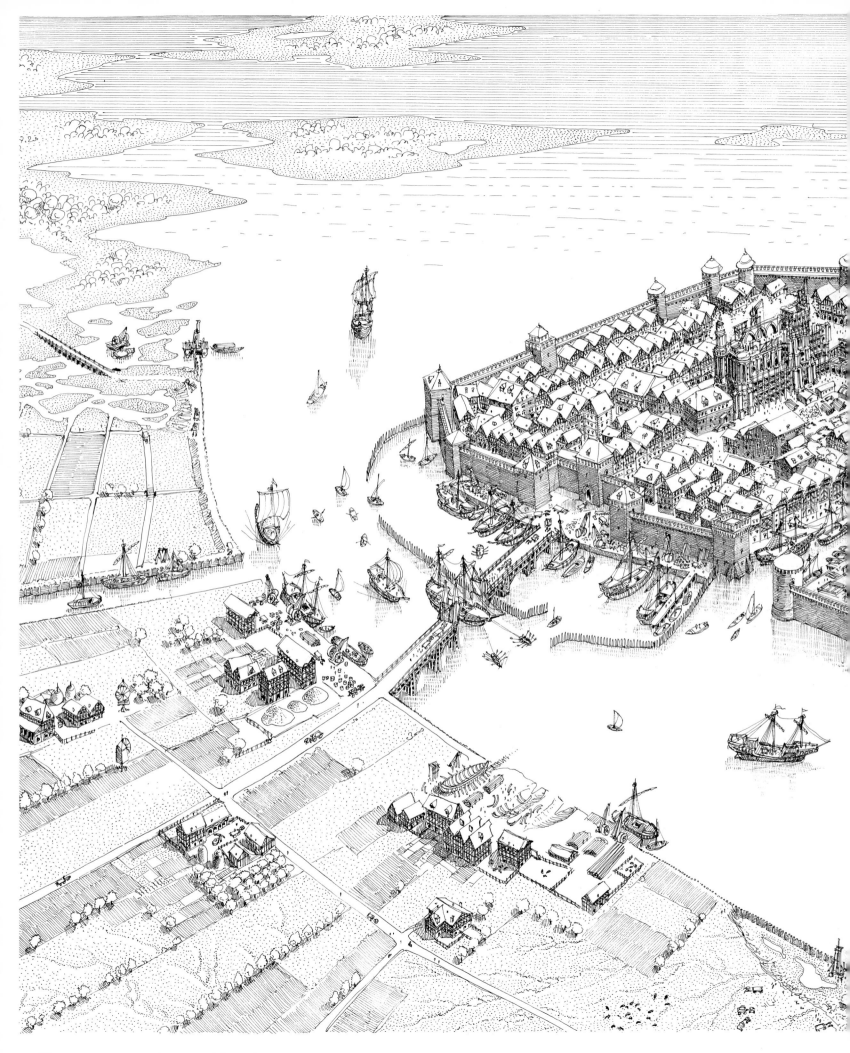

4. THE HERRING TOWN (mid - 14th century)

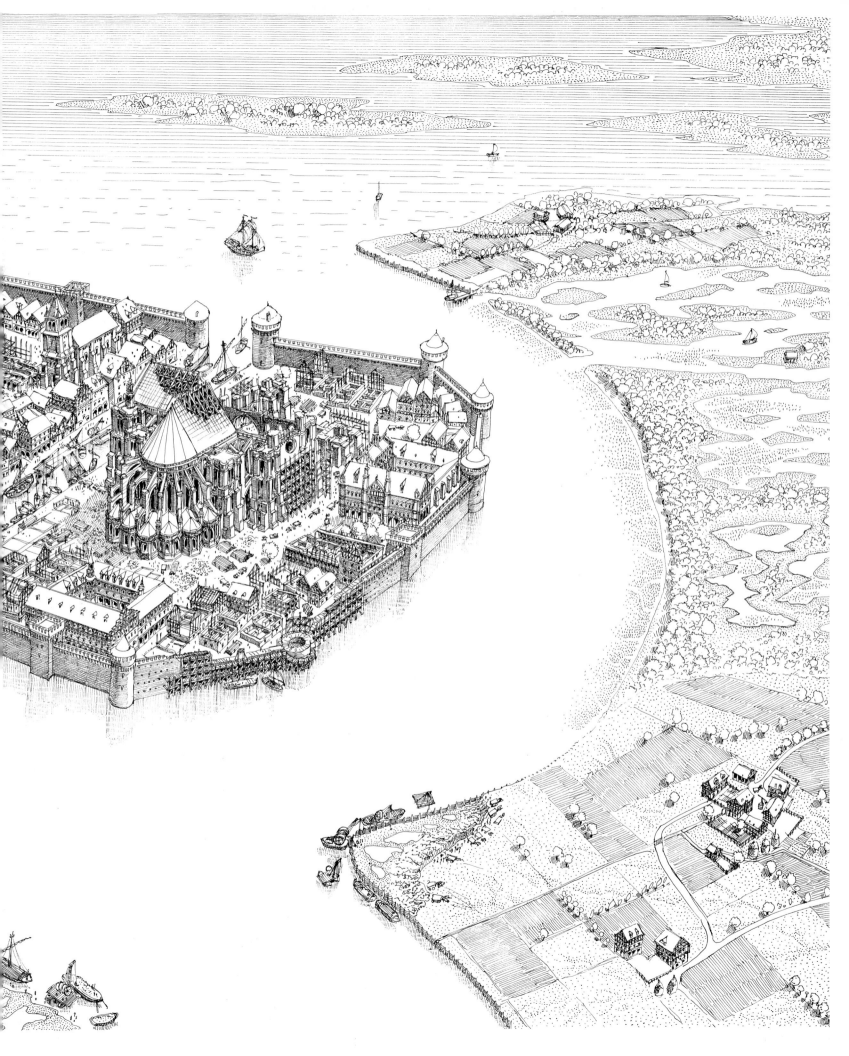

4. THE HERRING TOWN

(MID - 14TH CENTURY)

Lebek's prosperity continued to increase and, as in times gone by, trade was the driving force. On account of its convenient situation on the coast, the city was associated with the Hanseatic League, the large commercial organization that united the northern Germanic towns. But Lebek's trading links reached further afield; the city's merchants also maintained connections with the Flemish trading guild (in nearby Flanders) and had interests in Picardy and England.

All kinds of different ships from all over Europe sailed in and out of the port. They came from Genoa, Marseilles and Catalonia in the distant Mediterranean, bringing spices, alum, silk, glassware and wine. Large cargoes of salt arrived from the Atlantic coast of France, and from the Baltic countries came skins, iron, copper and wood, dried cod and smoked fish. In return, Lebek offered quantities of cloth woven in the city's workshops and from those in towns inland. From the higher reaches of the Leb came quantities of manufactured goods, weapons and cattle.

In addition to the wealth brought by this trade, the city also ran a prosperous sideline in salt herring. Like other coastal towns,

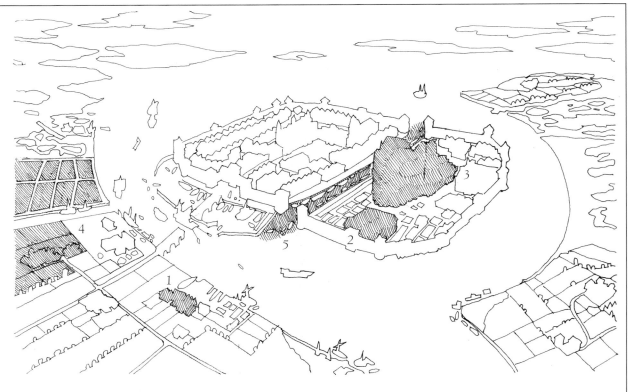

1. Herring-salting factories
Fishing fleets brought back quantities of herring from the Baltic and North Seas. The herring were cleaned straight away and, as soon as they were delivered to the factory, they were salted and packed into barrels. Smoking was another way of preserving fish, although less often used. The drying process was used mostly for cod.

2. The hospital
Hospitals, usually run by religious orders, improved the quality of life for citizens, taking care of the injured and coping with diseases and epidemics, common in seaports. Medieval doctors treated their patients with medical knowledge mixed with traditional folklore.

3. The cathedral
Tall Gothic cathedrals built in the style that had evolved in France and in Germany became the hallmark of northern European cities. Tall and slender, they were a magnificent sight. Building a cathedral was a process that took many years; several generations of stonemasons and architects were usually involved, each one adding new ideas to the original design.

4. Farmsteads
Meanwhile, the battle to win land back from the sea still went on outside the city. Despite great efforts, results were slow. Dykes had to be built, water drained off and land desalinated. Land on which to grow crops was gradually reclaimed and it was here that new farmsteads were built. But a storm, unusually high tides or flooding could destroy all this effort at a stroke.

5. The canal
Some lowland cities had canals running through them just like streets. They were convenient for getting about in the city centre and for moving goods about. They were also the city sewers. Large canals were also built between towns and rivers inland; this made transport by water more efficient than by road.

BUILDING A CATHEDRAL	1. Levelling the ground and digging the foundations
	2. Raising the walls, pillars, columns and buttresses of the apse
	3. Building the roof and the transept

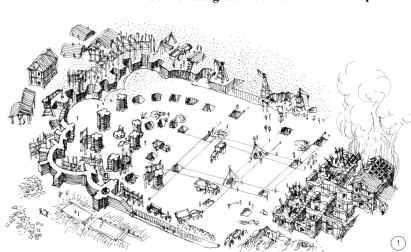

Lebek had a fishing fleet that brought in catches of herring which arrived in shoals off its southern coast. When the herrings were landed, they were salted and packed into barrels, where they remained perfectly preserved for about twelve months. Thousands of barrels were exported all over Europe, especially to Mediterranean towns. Because herrings were cheap, rich in protein and kept well, they provided an excellent diet for the townspeople of northern Europe, and saved the poorer classes from starvation. For Lebek, meanwhile, the shoals of herring contributed greatly to the expansion of the city and to its wealth.

As Lebek grew, new ramparts were built around it. Now the city covered the whole island. A wide canal, dividing the city into two, provided a convenient means of loading and unloading ships. A hospital run by a religious order of friars was built in the new suburbs. The prosperity of the times led to some ambitious projects. With the agreement of the Church, merchants and craftsmen financed the building of a great Gothic cathedral, as splendid and imposing as any that could be seen in northern Europe.

Major alterations were made to the market square, as work began on an imposing new guildhall that would reflect the importance and status of a free city. The most powerful guilds began to build palaces, which would serve as their headquarters. Old houses were gradually replaced by larger and more comfortable ones. The growth of Lebek was in full swing.

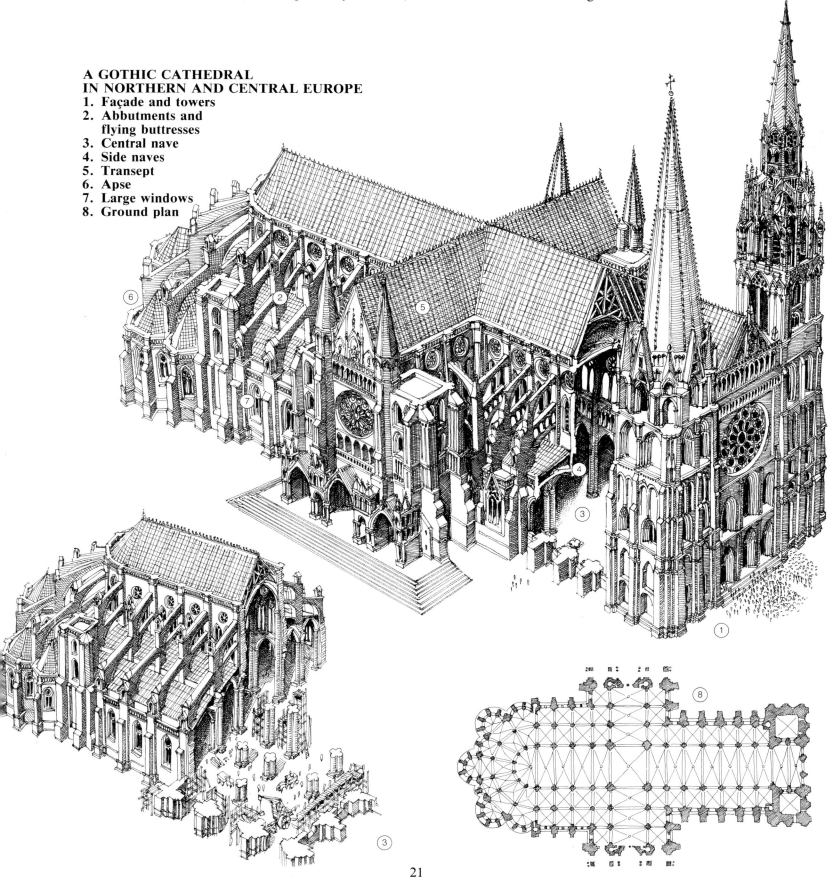

**A GOTHIC CATHEDRAL
IN NORTHERN AND CENTRAL EUROPE**
1. Façade and towers
2. Abbutments and
   flying buttresses
3. Central nave
4. Side naves
5. Transept
6. Apse
7. Large windows
8. Ground plan

5. A DECLINE IN TRADING POWER
(EARLY 16TH CENTURY)

Throughout the 15th century, the medieval city of Lebek continued to grow and prosper in spite of occasional periods of adversity. At the beginning of the 16th century, important buildings were still going up. The guildhall, the guild of wool merchants and the university were completed. The outskirts of the city now reached the left bank of the river and surrounded the dockyards and salting houses. Large and splendid three-masted ships were a common sight in the port, living proof of the city's importance and vitality.

But things had begun to change. The shoals of herring disappeared from the North Sea, bringing ruin to the fishing and curing industry. New alliances were being formed among the various Nordic kingdoms, and the rising powers of Sweden and Russia posed serious threats to northern trading towns like Lebek. European settlement in North America, and the increasing strength of other European nations, weakened the position of the northern free cities. Now, the

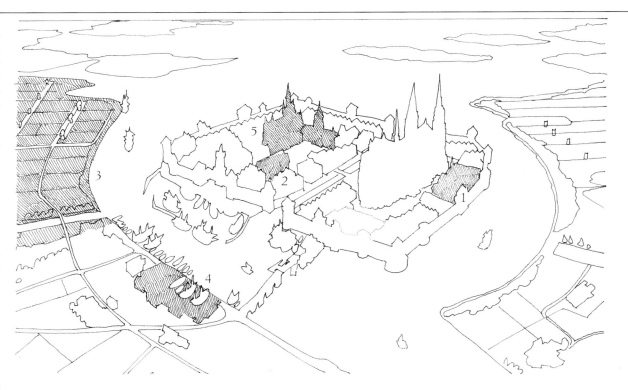

1. The university
The medieval-style universities taught very little that was of use to the advancement of trade and development of scientific knowledge. At this time science had nothing to do with economic progress; that happened much later. Theology, law, rhetoric, Greek, Latin and medicine were the usual subjects studied in universities.

2. The guilds
The most powerful tradesmen's and craftsmen's guilds built impressive headquarters for themselves. These elegant buildings housed documents and records and served as places where meetings and assemblies took place. The guilds were highly organized, having their own banners, festivals and traditions.

3. Canals, windmills and dykes
During the 15th century, the battle against the marshlands and the sea was stepped up. Land to be reclaimed was enclosed within a sturdy earth wall, or dyke, on which windmills were placed. The windmills drove Archimedean screws which lifted the water up and emptied it into rivers and canals outside the dyke. Dykes, dams and sluice gates protected and controlled the complicated network of canals.

4. Dockyards
By the early 16th century, ships were already large. These merchants' ships would soon be replaced by great four-masted galleons. Great technical skill and the availability of large quantities of wood were needed to build such ships. The dockyard therefore had to be well equipped to keep up with the demands of shipbuilding.

5. The Guildhall
At the beginning of the 16th century, the front of the guildhall was embellished to show off the power and wealth of the city. Renaissance and baroque details were added to these basically gothic buildings.

THE PORT
River boats, fishing boats, herring boats (busses) and great sea-going vessels, arriving from across the oceans, were moored alongside the quays. Goods were piled up along the wharves, ready to be stored away in nearby warehouses or loaded into the holds of ships.

1. Crane
2. Gangplank
3. Bundles of wool and barrels of salt herring
4. Merchant ship
5. Herring boat or buss

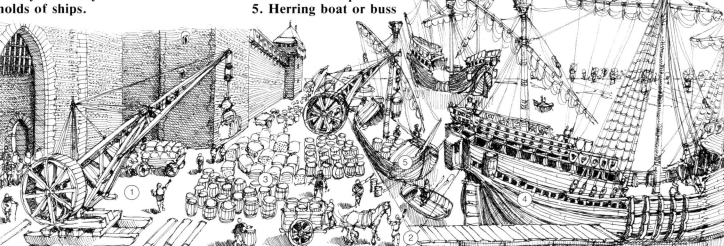

trading cities of the North and Baltic Seas, as well as the Mediterranean, lost their supremacy. The medieval world was disintegrating. From now on, the Atlantic Ocean was to play a leading role in shipping and communication.

The dukedom of the lower Leb now became part of a large foreign empire and Lebek lost much of its freedom. In an attempt to adjust to the new era, the city's merchants turned to establishing trading links across the oceans. However, finding new markets was not so easy. A few of the city's seafarers were bold enough to set off and explore unknown waters and trade routes to the West Indies, which were to be vitally important to them in the future.

Life in the city continued at a slower pace. The wool-weaving industry made the most of cheap imports of wool. A number of Lebek's merchants had turned to banking, and a share of the wealth of gold and silver now reaching Europe from the Americas ended up in the city.

The continual battle to maintain sea defences was much helped by new construction methods. In the 15th century, windmills had been systematically used to drain the marshes. Now, dykes were built to contain the sea and ditches were dug to channel water away from the marshlands. The network of canals was also improved as these new projects were begun. It seemed as if, by their determined efforts to improve the land around them, the people of the Leb estuary were making up for the trade they had lost.

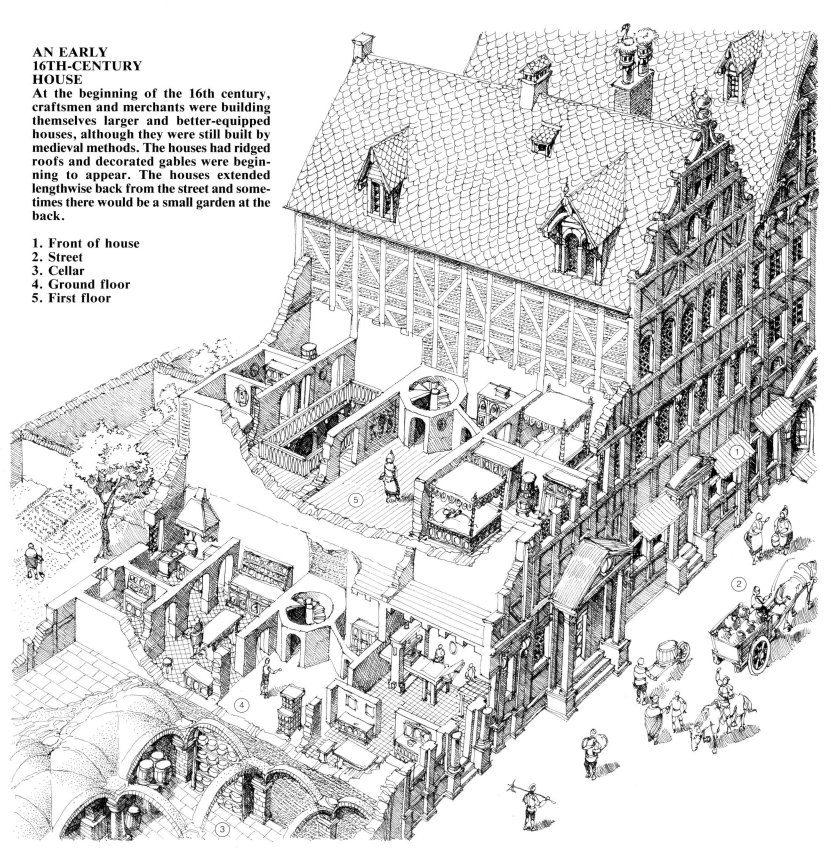

AN EARLY 16TH-CENTURY HOUSE

At the beginning of the 16th century, craftsmen and merchants were building themselves larger and better-equipped houses, although they were still built by medieval methods. The houses had ridged roofs and decorated gables were beginning to appear. The houses extended lengthwise back from the street and sometimes there would be a small garden at the back.

1. Front of house
2. Street
3. Cellar
4. Ground floor
5. First floor

6. RECLAIMING THE LAND (early 17th century)

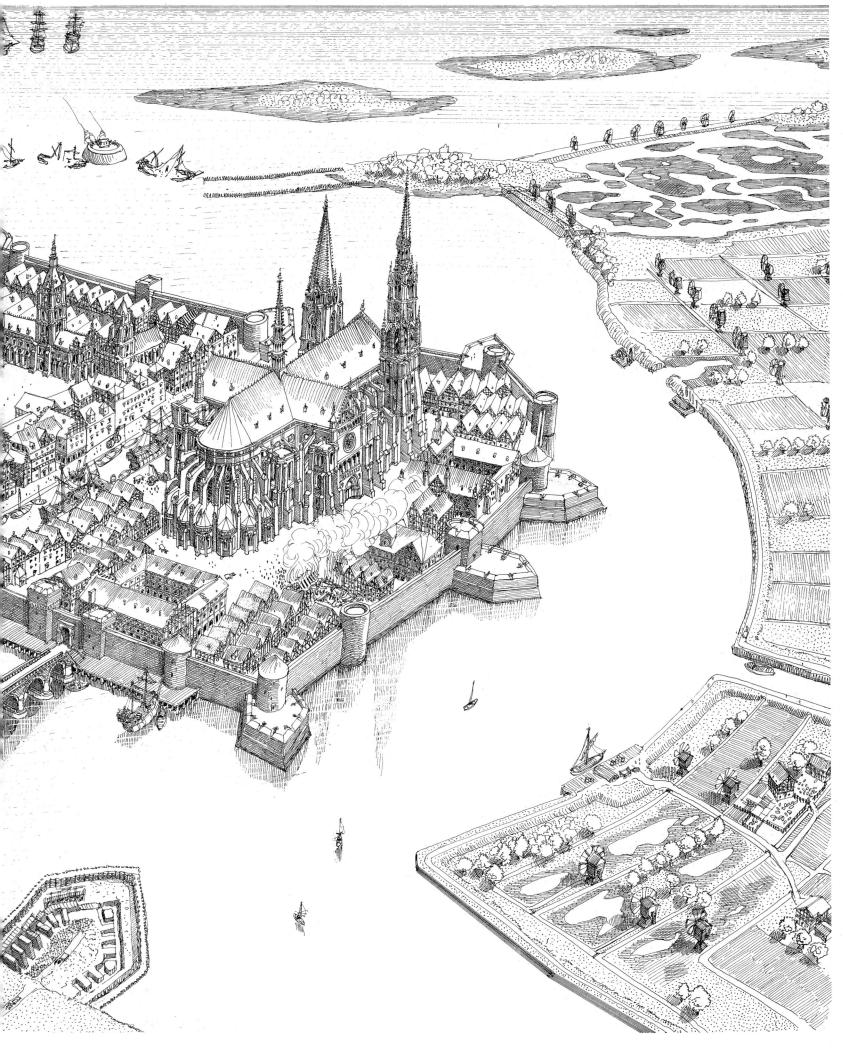

6. RECLAIMING THE LAND
(EARLY 17TH CENTURY)

By the mid-16th century, the pace of life was starting to quicken again in Lebek. Merchants here and in other coastal towns, were struggling to establish themselves in the East and West Indies, even resorting to piracy in the process. The bankers, meanwhile, were very active, borrowing and lending money and financing enterprises.

Efforts to control the sea were increased and more and more dykes were built and canals dug. Windmills turned day and night, provid-ing power to drain the marshlands and reclaim land for cultivation. The great network of canals, dykes, locks and drawbridges made com-munication much easier between the city and towns inland. The port of Lebek was enlarged and its defences were improved. It harboured trading ships, herring boats and various small craft. Pirate ships, hav-ing intercepted Spanish galleons carrying gold and silver from the Americas, also found a haven there.

Whaling became an important industry and trade in whale oil for fuel and whalebone for corsets and other items brought in consider-able revenue. The city began to grow again. For the first time in its history, the island-town was permanently connected to the mainland by a stone bridge. The outskirts of the city spread out over the river-

1. Windmills
During the 16th and especially in the 17th century, years of ex-perience led to the improvement of windmills in order to get the most out of wind power. Many windmills worked to drain water from the lowlands. They were also used to mill grain.

2. Building dykes
When a piece of land was to be reclaimed, the first thing to do was build a dyke right around it. The dyke was built up with earth dug from the outside of the boundary; this helped to provide a canal to take the water away. The dyke was made of earth, silt, branches and bram-bles. Windmills were installed along the top. Waterlogged land had to be drained by a series of windmills.

3. Flooded fields
Storms sometimes destroyed dykes and dams. Then the fields would be under water again. But flooding the fields could also be a man-made decision. During times of war, dykes and dams were often destroyed, allowing water to pour in and flood the fields. This voluntary flooding created an effective barrier against invading armies.

4. Bastions in city walls
In the post-medieval period, new walls were built incorporating bastions. This was where the ar-tillery was placed, ready to defend the city and port from the approaching enemy. Wide ditches, often filled with water, surrounded the steep-sided walls, to make another obstacle for the enemy to overcome.

5. Siege trenches
If a city was to be taken, the walls had to be breached. The at-tacking army dug deep trenches in a zig-zag in front of the walls. From these trenches, the attack-ing artillery tried to open a breach in the walls. The foot soldiers meanwhile advanced to the breach and tried to enter the city.

DYKES, CANALS, WINDMILLS
In order to drain away the lower water, a series of windmills were used to power the Archimed-ean screws. The water was conveyed progressively up to the higher drainage canals. From here the top mills controlled the water, allowing it to pour into the rivers, or, by means of a sluice gate, straight into the sea at low tide.

1. Limit of high tide
2. Limit of low tide
3. Dyke
4. Mills
5. Drainage canals

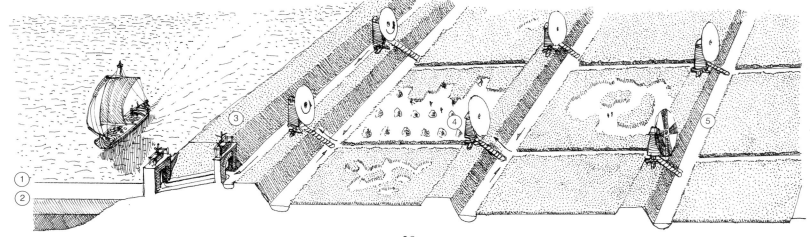

The rise of Britain as a naval power created some difficulties; squabbles broke out over who should have control of fishing rights. Lebek was the winner in this struggle because of its strong naval superiority.

Meanwhile, in the city's workshops, woollen cloth was still being woven and many craftsmen were employed on engineering projects. The city continued to grow, both outwards and upwards. The outskirts were now completely built up. Within the safety of the walls, work in the dockyard progressed fast; more and more ships were being built to defend the country's trade routes. Because of the deep water of the estuary, huge sea-going vessels could be launched from the dockyard.

An imposing building — one of the finest modern banks in Europe — was built. Here, all kinds of business deals took place. Soon almost all the open spaces on the outskirts of the city were covered by the houses of craftsmen and merchants.

The appearance of the houses in the ancient city centre also changed. Because there was no room for them to expand outwards, they grew upwards. New, ornately decorated, timbered façades were a clear sign that this was a prosperous and important town.

As the countryside recovered from the ravages of war, people worked to put right the damage that had been done to the land. Agriculture, livestock and dairy produce flourished. Lebek was now enjoying one of the richest periods in its history.

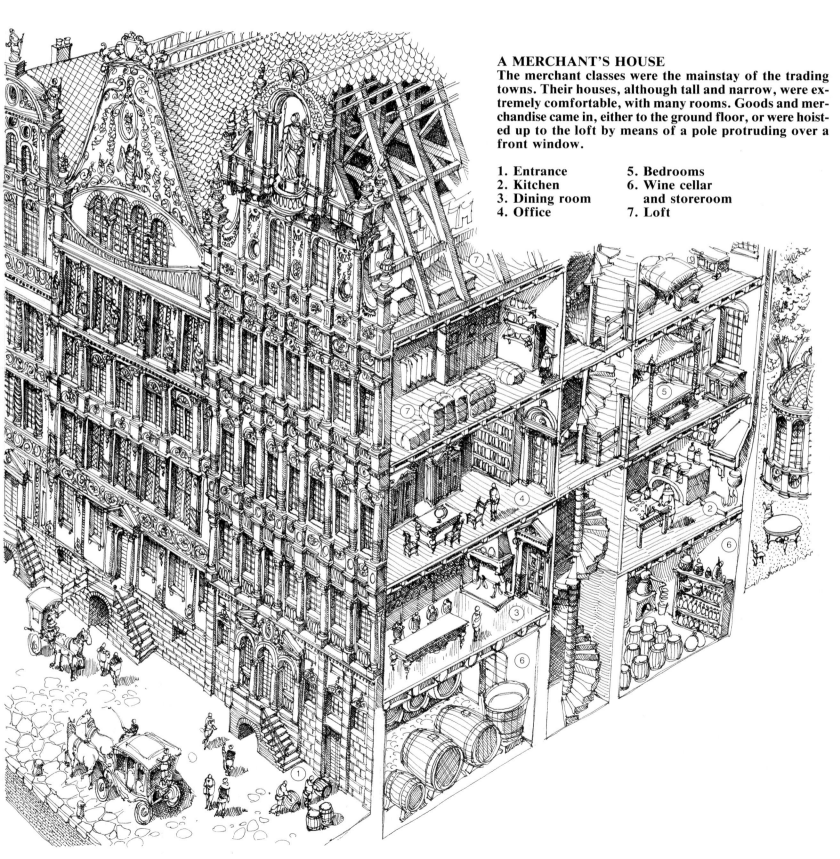

A MERCHANT'S HOUSE

The merchant classes were the mainstay of the trading towns. Their houses, although tall and narrow, were extremely comfortable, with many rooms. Goods and merchandise came in, either to the ground floor, or were hoisted up to the loft by means of a pole protruding over a front window.

1. Entrance
2. Kitchen
3. Dining room
4. Office
5. Bedrooms
6. Wine cellar and storeroom
7. Loft

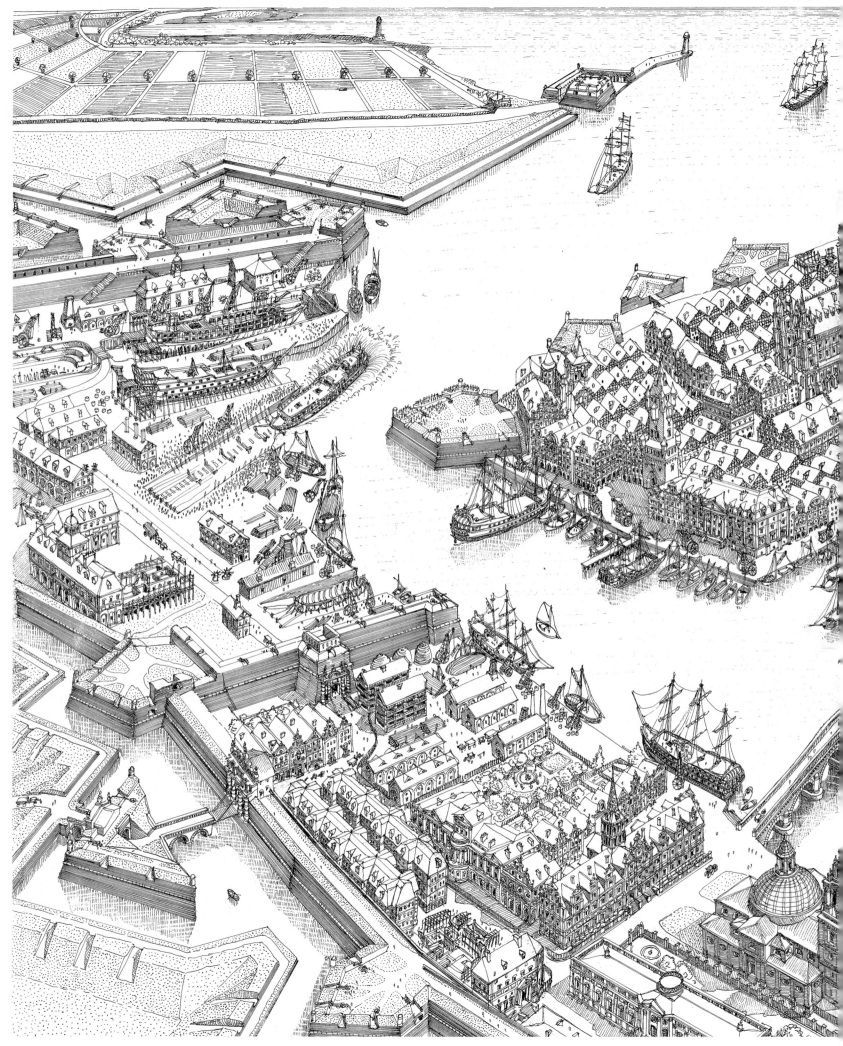

8. THE FORTIFIED CITY AND PORT (mid - 18th century)

8. THE FORTIFIED CITY AND PORT
(MID-18TH CENTURY)

The complex political situation of the countries of northern and central Europe during the 18th century, combined with continual wars, were to play a key part in shaping the modern city of Lebek.

At this time the city seemed to barricade itself against the outside world. The walls were increasingly strengthened and set with fortifications, built using the newest French methods. Although the city still kept its old character as a great seaport and trading centre, it had become a fortress.

Piracy was a thing of the past and naval ships now patrolled the waters off Lebek. Shipbuilding continued as actively as before, and ever larger ships were built in the dockyard, under the direction of the city governors. Great arsenals were built for the navy and the dockyard became an enclosed world within the city. It had its own fortifications, isolating it from the outside world and from the city itself. All kinds of storehouses and workshops provided essential

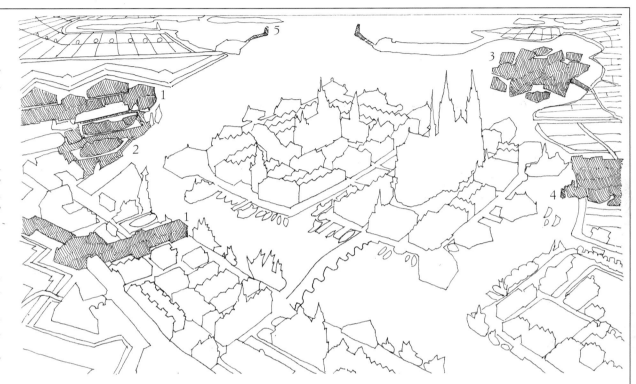

1. Ramparts round the naval dockyard
Naval dockyards were practically self-sufficient units, with different sorts of storehouses and workshops. Because of their military purpose, they were isolated, protected and quite independent of ports and cities.

2. A dry dock
Dry docks, with their complex workings, were costly to build but without them it would have been impossible to repair and maintain large vessels on dry land.

3. City strongholds
During the 18th century military engineering made great progress in the construction of fortifications. Additional strongholds were added to safeguard the flanks of the central fortress, making sure that it was well defended.

4. A coal yard
At the beginning of the 18th century, coal was usually carried by ship. Ships specially built for this purpose, with large holds and extra-strong hulls, were loaded with coal from raised conveyor belts.

5. The lighthouse
*Lighthouses aided navigation and helped ships to reach and enter the port. Some were float-*ing lighthouses. These allowed ships to enter and leave the port at night and negotiate the complex estuary channels.

METALWORKING IN THE NAVAL DOCKYARD

Hundreds of craftsmen with special skills could be seen working in the great naval dockyard. Carpenters, caulkers and shipwrights took care of boatbuilding. Ropemakers, producing all sorts of rope, worked in large sheds with all the equipment needed for twisting lengths of hawser. Sculptors, woodworkers, and decorators added the finishing touches to the ships. Casting and forging metal was the most important work in the dockyard. Cannons and other weapons were forged and all kinds of ships' fittings were produced.

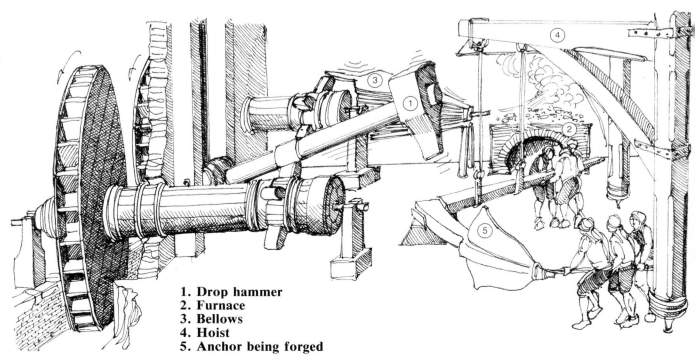

1. **Drop hammer**
2. **Furnace**
3. **Bellows**
4. **Hoist**
5. **Anchor being forged**

equipment for maintaining and fitting out the navy; there was a foundry, for the forging of anchors and other iron implements, and a rope works where strong rope was produced.

The dockyard was equipped with stocks for conventional shipbuilding, but its most important feature was a great dry dock. As well as being used for building ships, the dry dock was useful when ships needed to be repaired. The sluice gates were closed and the water in the dock was emptied out by means of pumps and waterwheels. The caulkers and shipwrights then set to work.

Other industrial developments in Lebek were in the cloth-weaving industry. Workshops were grouped together into factories, and, although they still depended on traditional methods, these factories streamlined production. The craftsmen who worked in them were becoming the first industrial wage earners.

Technical advances in metalworking, leading to the need for greater furnaces, also indirectly affected Lebek. Boats laden with coal from collieries up-river, sailed down to the port. Ships especially designed to carry coal, loaded up their cargo and carried it off to iron and steel-making foundries.

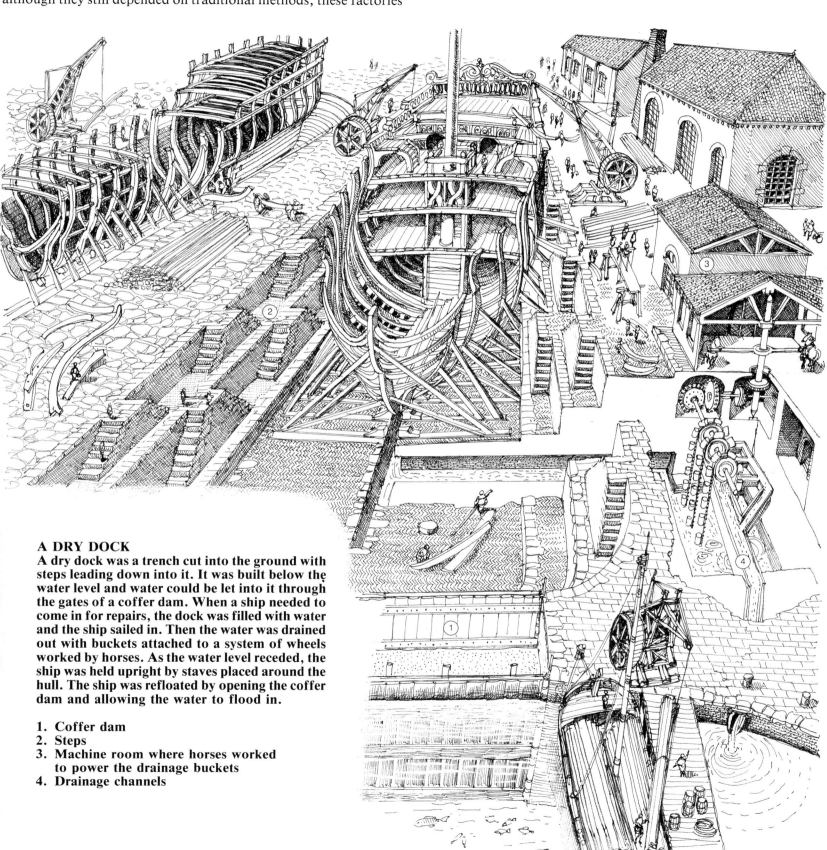

A DRY DOCK
A dry dock was a trench cut into the ground with steps leading down into it. It was built below the water level and water could be let into it through the gates of a coffer dam. When a ship needed to come in for repairs, the dock was filled with water and the ship sailed in. Then the water was drained out with buckets attached to a system of wheels worked by horses. As the water level receded, the ship was held upright by staves placed around the hull. The ship was refloated by opening the coffer dam and allowing the water to flood in.

1. **Coffer dam**
2. **Steps**
3. **Machine room where horses worked to power the drainage buckets**
4. **Drainage channels**

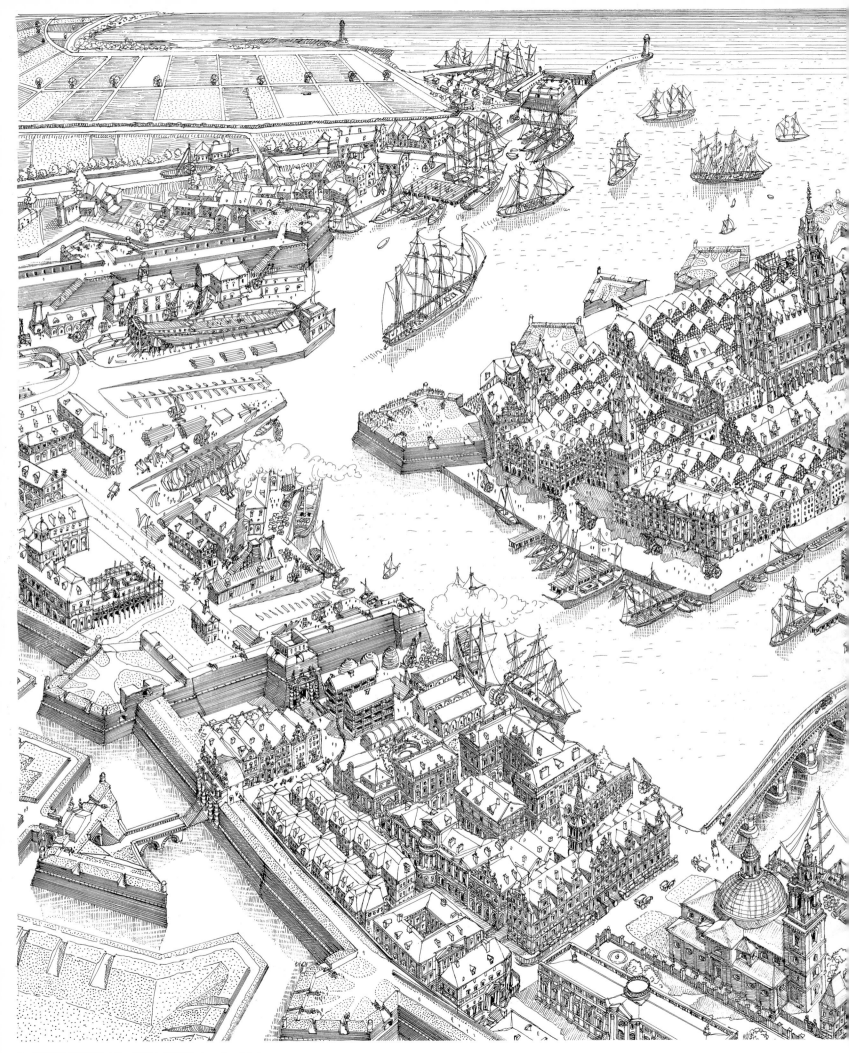

9. INDUSTRIAL CHANGE (early 19th century)

9. INDUSTRIAL CHANGE
(EARLY 19TH CENTURY)

ing scientific and technological advances of the 19th century that were to transform the urban landscape of Europe. Developments in the iron and steel industry, the first steam-driven machines and the gradual mechanization of the textile industry all led to rapid changes.

Lebek began to expand again. The city walls, now little more than an old circle of stones, no longer protected the city. Instead, they threatened to stifle it.

Although the traditional industries of fish-curing and the weaving of wool were still important, the port now expanded to take in other industries. Cargoes of coal continued to arrive from the interior, to satisfy ever-increasing demand. And, as a result of overseas trade, all kinds of exotic goods — tea, coffee, sugar, tropical hardwoods

During the late 18th century and into the first decades of the 19th century, the city of Lebek slumbered on as if it were resting before another burst of expansion. However, revolutions and a fresh spirit of freedom were bringing Europe into a new age. But it was the amaz-

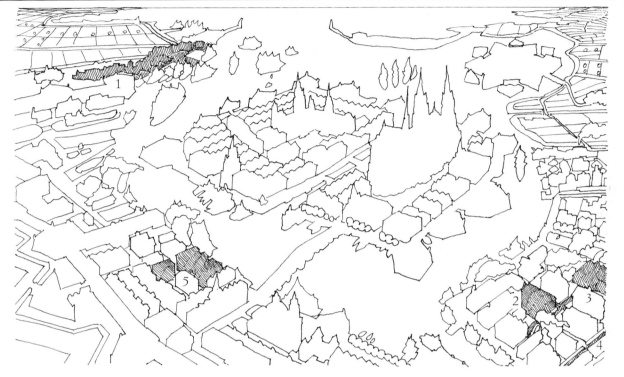

1. New quays
Increased volumes of shipping in the port — the result of combined activity on the part of the European colonial powers — led to the need for new quays that could accommodate increasingly large ships. The section of the port immediately behind the quays was given over to the needs of seamen and their vessels.

2. Factories
The first factories attracted large numbers of employees. Factory owners paid a wage in return for labour. To begin with, in spite of this new method of production, traditional methods, machines and sources of energy continued to be used. Some guilds — especially those connected with the textile industry, which was ideal for industrialization — were destroyed by competition from large factories.

3. Workers' estates
Factories became the hallmark of a town, just as churches and castles had been in times gone by. Housing for the workers sprang up around the factories. At the same time, some houses in the poorest parts of the city expanded upwards to accommodate the increasing numbers of workers.

4. Aqueduct
In flat or low-lying areas, water power was too weak to turn the water wheels that worked the factories' machinery. Aqueducts had to be built to bring water from a higher level further afield. This provided a current strong enough to move the waterwheels. The raised canals

brought water that worked several different mills.

5. New buildings in the city
The rise of the neo-classical style in Europe was seen particularly clearly in public buildings such as colleges, chambers of commerce and headquarters for overseas trade, banks and the

houses of the nobility and of prosperous merchants and factory owners.

A WATER WHEEL
Slopes were needed to provide enough power for waterwheels to move machinery. The rivers, slowly meandering across the flat lowlands, could not produce enough power to turn waterwheels, so to obtain a strong current of water, canals had to be built to bring water down from a higher level.
Where there was a gentle slope, a waterwheel was used to make the most of the water current. Paddle boards of the correct shape and size, placed at a certain angle to the water could make a dramatic difference to the mill's efficiency. As the axle of the water wheel turned it also turned the cog wheels, which then moved the machines in the factory.

1. Waterwheel
2. Workshops
3. Skylights for natural lighting
4. Bell for the start and finish of shifts

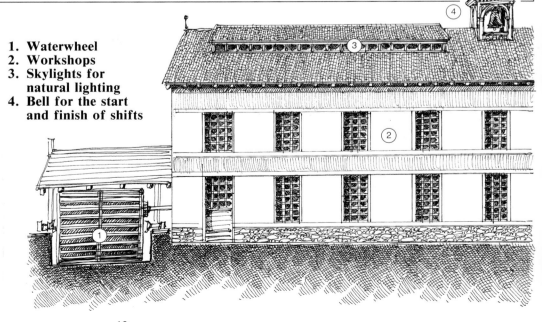

and, notably, bundles of raw cotton — arrived at the port in growing quantities from distant colonies. Cotton weaving soon became the leading industry in Lebek. New factories for spinning and weaving appeared and the woven cloth was immediately re-exported to distant markets.

Although few changes could be made in the cramped city centre, some of the houses were altered, and public buildings were modernized or rebuilt to house large institutions such as banks.

Outside the city walls, new docks were built to take the increased shipping in the port. Nearby, a huddle of inns, lodging houses, shops and stores connected with shipworkers and shipping, made up the dockworkers' district.

Space for the new cotton mills also had to be found outside the walls. To enable the factories to use modern machinery, an aqueduct was built to carry water to them from a lake in the distant highlands to the south. Through the aqueduct flowed water to power the wheels, which in turn worked the mechanical looms.

Scattered untidily around the factories, the first workers' ghettoes formed. Lebek was being turned into an industrial town and a modern seaport. The city's industry was becoming more important than its trade.

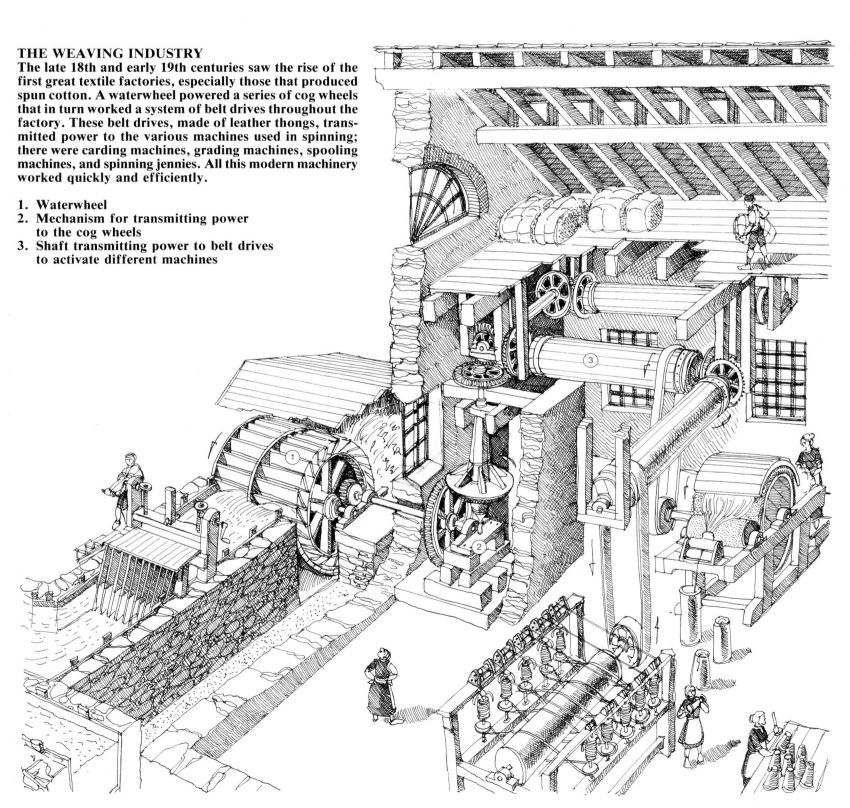

THE WEAVING INDUSTRY
The late 18th and early 19th centuries saw the rise of the first great textile factories, especially those that produced spun cotton. A waterwheel powered a series of cog wheels that in turn worked a system of belt drives throughout the factory. These belt drives, made of leather thongs, transmitted power to the various machines used in spinning; there were carding machines, grading machines, spooling machines, and spinning jennies. All this modern machinery worked quickly and efficiently.

1. **Waterwheel**
2. **Mechanism for transmitting power to the cog wheels**
3. **Shaft transmitting power to belt drives to activate different machines**

10. THE STEAM AGE (mid - 19th century)

10. THE STEAM AGE
(MID - 19TH CENTURY)

Around the mid-19th century, Lebek began to change quickly. New technology, methods of production and transport, all of which had developed rapidly since steam power came into general use, took dramatic steps forward.

The old factories, once worked by water, were now converted to steam power as the standard source of energy, and new factories, also using steam, were built all over the city. These factories, with their tall, smoking chimneys, producing a whole range of goods, became the new symbol for the city. They gradually covered all the green fields around Lebek.

Factory workers, who had come from the countryside in their hundreds, made up the bulk of the working population. They lived in specially-built workers' estates, which were arranged in rectangular blocks and situated around the factories.

Industrialization also affected other parts of the city. The outer corners of the old city walls were knocked down and the arsenal, now

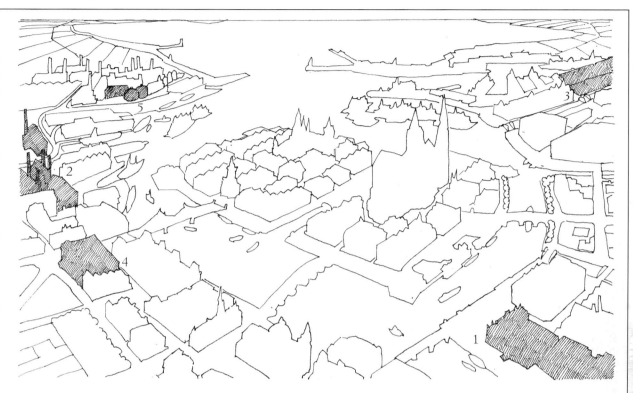

1. Railway station
Railway lines running straight into the city centre made replanning essential. Trains provided cheap and quick transport, both of goods and people. In a seaport, trains ensured that freight was delivered swiftly.

2. Steam-powered factories
The building of large factories with steam-driven machinery for the textile and other industries, had a dramatic effect on the look of mid-19th century towns and cities. Steam engines brought mechanization to industry and dramatically speeded up production.

3. Workers' estates
Factory owners sometimes provided housing for their workers, often building on their own land near the factory. Housing estates, consisting of parallel streets and rows of houses back-to-back, became an increasingly common sight in industrialized cities.

4. Business and commerce
A business centre developed far from the grime of the factories
and the bustle of the port. Banks, service industries and other businesses were set up here. A number of middle-class people moved to new houses in this part of the city.

5. The gas works
Gas came into general use around the mid-19th century. A complex network of underground pipes brought gas to street lamps. Comfortable
homes all had gas light. So did most factories, where work could now continue through the night.

STEAM POWER IN THE FACTORY
Burning coal in a furnace underneath a large boiler made enough heat to produce steam. The smoke from the coal fire escaped through a tall chimney. The steam, under pressure, was channelled through pipes to a steam engine. The engine worked a piston which in turn worked a large fly wheel. A chain of cog wheels powered by the fly wheel, worked the belt drive that powered all the factory's machinery.

1. Chimney
2. Boiler
3. Furnace
4. Steam engine
5. Fly wheel
6. Belt drive

completely outdated, was destroyed to make way for more factories. The old city outskirts were swallowed up by housing for the workers.

Iron, produced in the modern foundries, became very important in construction, especially for bridge-building. Railway lines ran into the port and the city. Trains carrying passengers and large amounts of freight, swiftly and efficiently, provided an alternative to river transport.

Steam power also had an important effect on shipping. Although efforts were made to improve the speed and efficiency of sailing ships, they were inevitably overtaken by modern iron-hulled steam ships. The port was clearly unsuited to the design and draught of the new ships, and inadequate for the fast-growing volume of traffic. While

new docks with wide berths were built out into the sea, the river mouth was widened, with many more channels to protect the port from flooding.

Industrialization in Lebek had created a new and influential section of society, made up of the new factory owners, entrepreneurs and those from the merchant and professional classes. The residential areas that these people were building for themselves developed quickly.

There were also new amenities for the city. A gasworks provided heat and light for homes, a sewage system was installed, and lastly, running water was piped from lakes inland, putting an end to the old practice of drawing water from the river.

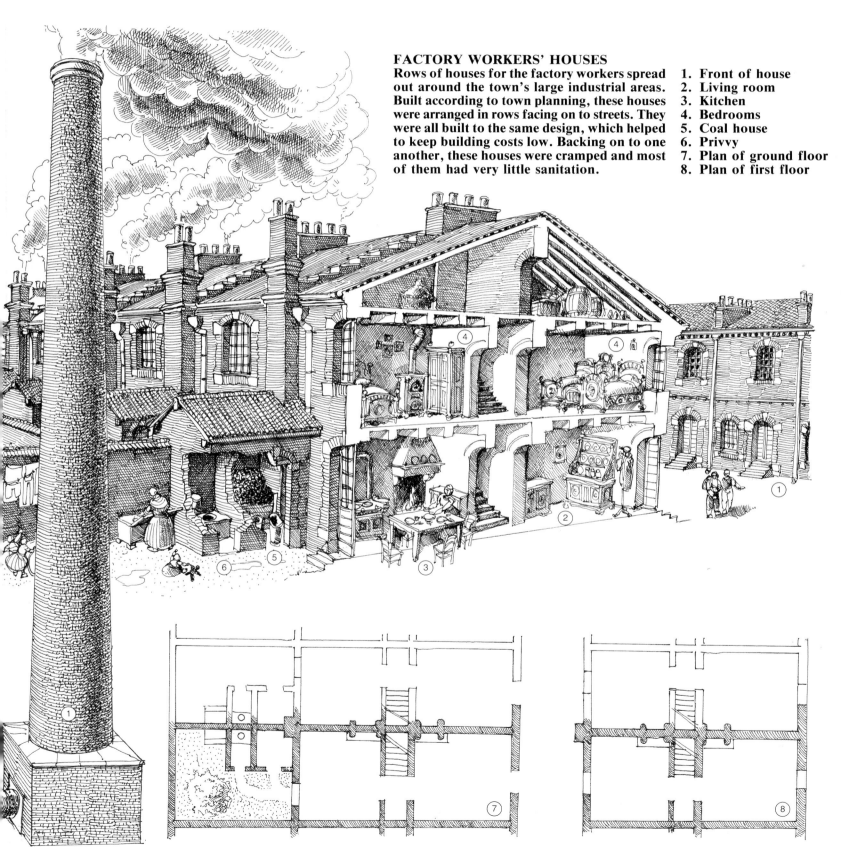

FACTORY WORKERS' HOUSES

Rows of houses for the factory workers spread out around the town's large industrial areas. Built according to town planning, these houses were arranged in rows facing on to streets. They were all built to the same design, which helped to keep building costs low. Backing on to one another, these houses were cramped and most of them had very little sanitation.

1. Front of house
2. Living room
3. Kitchen
4. Bedrooms
5. Coal house
6. Privvy
7. Plan of ground floor
8. Plan of first floor

11. A MAJOR SEAPORT (early 20th century)

11. A MAJOR SEAPORT
(EARLY 20TH CENTURY)

At the turn of the century, industrialization continued unabated. Electricity, as an alternative to steam power, and the internal combustion engine, both opened up exciting new possibilities. Electricity allowed industry to become more diverse because it was no longer dependent on access to central stockpiles of coal.

Besides being a major seaport and industrial centre, Lebek was also the centre of an important mining and iron and steel-making area, which stretched from the coastline far into the interior. This industrial area added to Lebek's importance, both as a centre of production and for trade and transport, since the port was vital for trade and communication.

Two large electricity generating plants now provided power for houses and factories; electric trams had been introduced, making transport into the city easier, and the first cars and buses were seen in the streets.

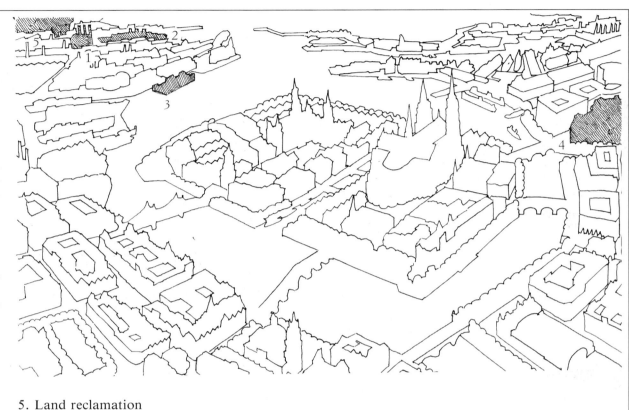

1. Power station
Large towns and cities without access to hydroelectric power had their own power stations, which provided electricity for the city and its immediate surroundings.

2. Naval dockyards
Potential conflict between the great European powers — the result of disputes over colonial lands — made it wise to build more and better warships. All kinds of wartime craft were designed and built in the great naval dockyards.

3. Floating docks
Floating docks could be raised and lowered at will, so that ships could be taken on board and raised up out of the water. Repairs and maintenance work could then be carried out.

4. New municipal buildings
As the city grew, public services needed central organization. New hospitals, schools, a fire service, tram depots, libraries and museums all became essential parts of the city.

5. Land reclamation
The development of cement and steel building technology made new construction and engineering techniques possible.

BUILDING WITH IRON
Advances in metalworking meant that iron and steel were now cheap and widely available building materials. Cast iron also began to be widely used. These advances in building materials led to dramatic developments in architecture. Instead of wooden beams, iron joists were used in the construction of buildings. Iron was also used for colonnades, balustrades and staircases.
A style of architecture especially suited to cast iron also evolved. It was seen at its best in grand public architecture and in buildings such as market halls, pavilions and warehouses.
Right: a pavilion for exhibitions built completely of cast iron.

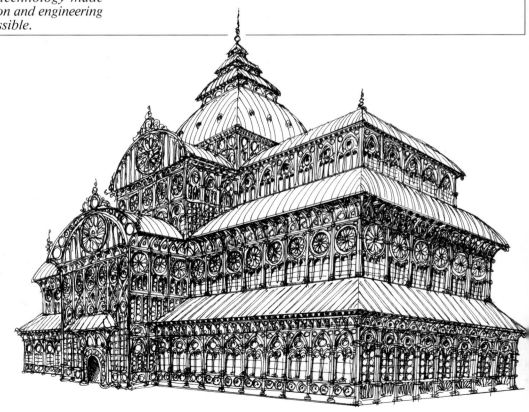

The workers housing estates continued to grow, spreading out over an ever-larger area. Splendid new buildings including offices for major banks and shipping and insurance companies, became the city's new landmarks.

The port, a vital link with the interior, underwent further expansion at this time. New harbours led to more dockyards and modern floating docks, where maintenance work could be carried out on ships. Huge stores of coal and fuel tanks for modern, oil-powered ships became part of the landscape of the port.

As the leading European powers went to war in 1914, warships were needed, and Lebek's traditional naval importance was revived. A huge dry dock, large enough for the biggest warships of the time, was built by the navy. Once again, just as the old arsenal used to hum with activity, hundreds of workers and engineers thronged the dockyard.

At the same time, work began again on reclaiming land from the sea. Under orders from the city council, engineers strengthened the sea walls, installed new dykes and gradually reclaimed the land. Very large areas were saved for agriculture. The old windmills were replaced by powerful pumping stations, and dykes were strengthened with steel and concrete and by new building techniques.

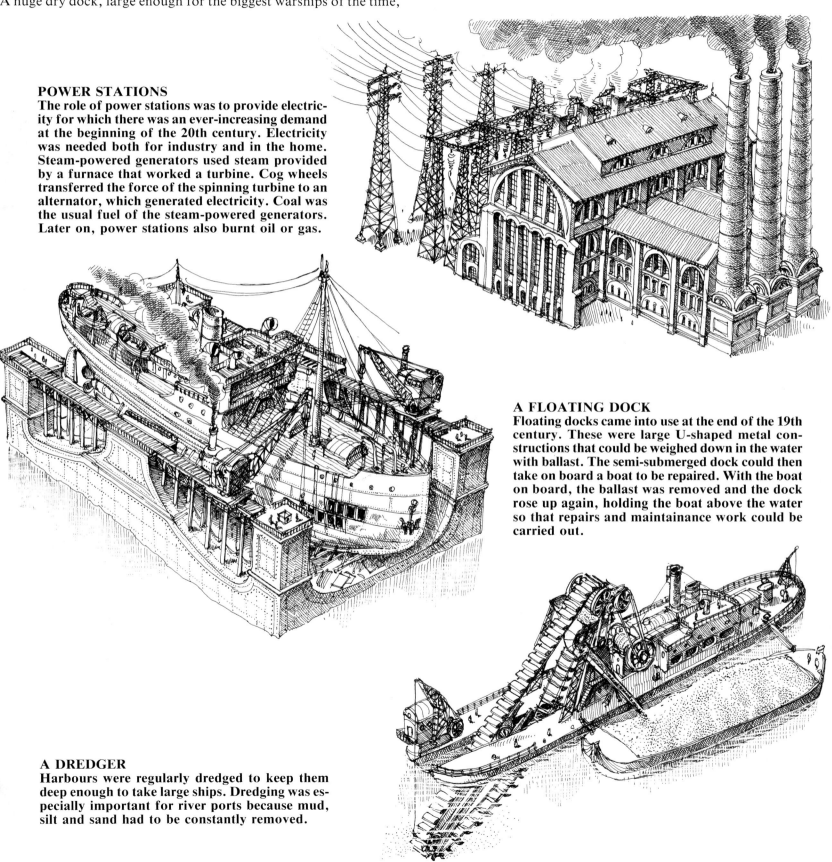

POWER STATIONS
The role of power stations was to provide electricity for which there was an ever-increasing demand at the beginning of the 20th century. Electricity was needed both for industry and in the home. Steam-powered generators used steam provided by a furnace that worked a turbine. Cog wheels transferred the force of the spinning turbine to an alternator, which generated electricity. Coal was the usual fuel of the steam-powered generators. Later on, power stations also burnt oil or gas.

A FLOATING DOCK
Floating docks came into use at the end of the 19th century. These were large U-shaped metal constructions that could be weighed down in the water with ballast. The semi-submerged dock could then take on board a boat to be repaired. With the boat on board, the ballast was removed and the dock rose up again, holding the boat above the water so that repairs and maintainance work could be carried out.

A DREDGER
Harbours were regularly dredged to keep them deep enough to take large ships. Dredging was especially important for river ports because mud, silt and sand had to be constantly removed.

12. DEVASTATION AND REBIRTH (2nd World War - 1939-45)

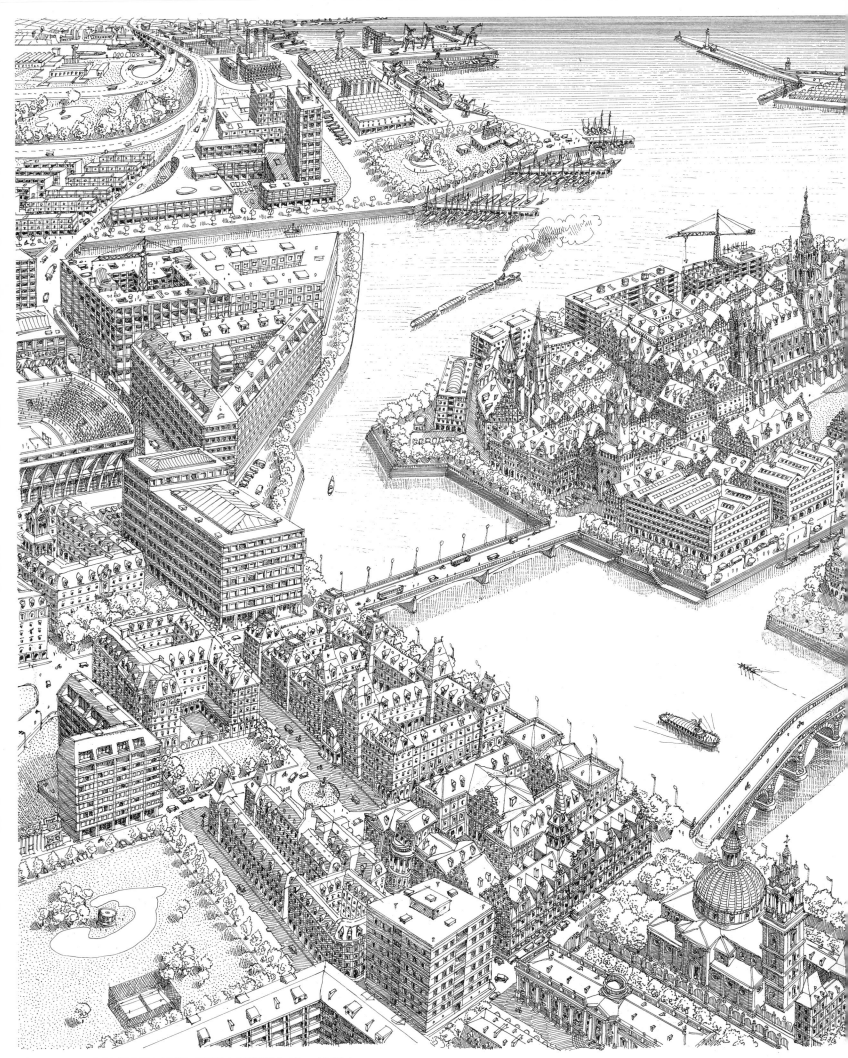

13. DEVELOPMENT AND EXPANSION (the 1960s)

13. DEVELOPMENT AND EXPANSION

(THE 1960s)

Very little happened in Lebek during the immediate post-war years. The whole of Europe was concentrating on repairing the ravages of the war. Although the city received aid in the form of money and equipment from other countries, the progress made in the process of recovery in Lebek was due to the hard work and determination of its citizens.

The rebuilding of Lebek began straight away. Within a few months the port had been tidied up and the dockyards gradually rebuilt. These were essential to shipping, which though scarce at first, eventually returned to its pre-war volume. The port was completely rebuilt, with a new phase of development beginning in the 1950s.

In the city, the bomb sites were cleared so that rebuilding could commence. The city was to be planned with future development in mind. The industrial areas, which had been completely destroyed during the war, were rebuilt further away from the centre, making room for shops and housing. The city became more spacious now that the crowded slums of earlier times were no longer tolerated. Wider streets, sports stadiums and centres for the arts now

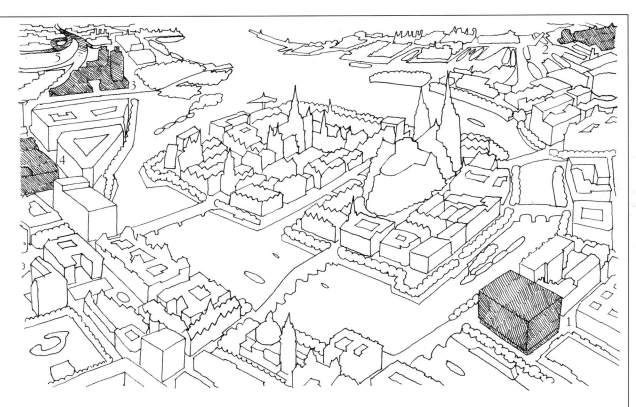

1. The municipal and commercial centre
New shopping precincts, offices and service departments were built in newly developed areas that had once been slums.

2. New industrial estates
Industry in the city centre, largely destroyed during the war, was moved to estates outside the city centre. They were equipped with everything that was needed for an efficient working environment.

3. Satellite towns
The growing population, particularly of people in lower income groups, was rehoused in new areas that were almost secondary towns outside the city.

4. Sport and entertainment amenities
Football grounds, sports centres, swimming pools, libraries, new museums and other amenities improved the quality of life in the city both in sport and cultural pursuits.

5. New roads and railways
The problem of access was a direct result of the city's growth. *New railway networks, ring roads and motorways had to be built to cope with the relentless* *and increasing volume of traffic in and out of the city and the port.*

A BLOCK OF FLATS
Many blocks of flats were built, mostly in newly developed areas of the city, but also in some parts of the old city centre. They were usually built to a set pattern and some parts were also prefabricated. Because ground space was scarce, building flats, one on top of the other in tall blocks, provided the solution to the pressing need for relatively cheap housing.

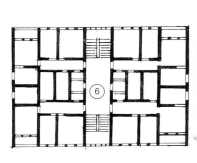

took priority in the municipal building programme.

The railway lines which used to cut right through the city were now re-routed around the outskirts, to the port. As cars and buses became more numerous, measures were taken to reduce the problem of traffic congestion.

Throughout the 1960s, the whole of industrialized Europe went through a major period of economic growth, which led to more specialized industries. Lebek, only just rebuilt, began to expand again. More industrial estates sprang up, and the port grew faster than ever, expanding outwards into the sea. The complex was now dominated by a new oil storage terminal, which stood at the mouth of the river. Freight that had previously been brought by barge was now carried by train or travelled on the system of trunk roads that linked the port and the city.

More poor housing areas — consisting of huge blocks of high-rise flats — appeared on the outskirts of the city. Generally however, improved sanitation, gas and electricity supplies provided a reasonable standard of living, unlike many other towns in Europe, where straggling slums often sprawled untidily. New hospitals, schools, sports stadiums and arts centres appeared as building continued, and the quality of life steadily improved in the city. But in spite of these improvements Lebek faced the usual problems of air pollution, damage to the environment, lack of space to expand, traffic congestion and the whole range of problems that go with life in a large city.

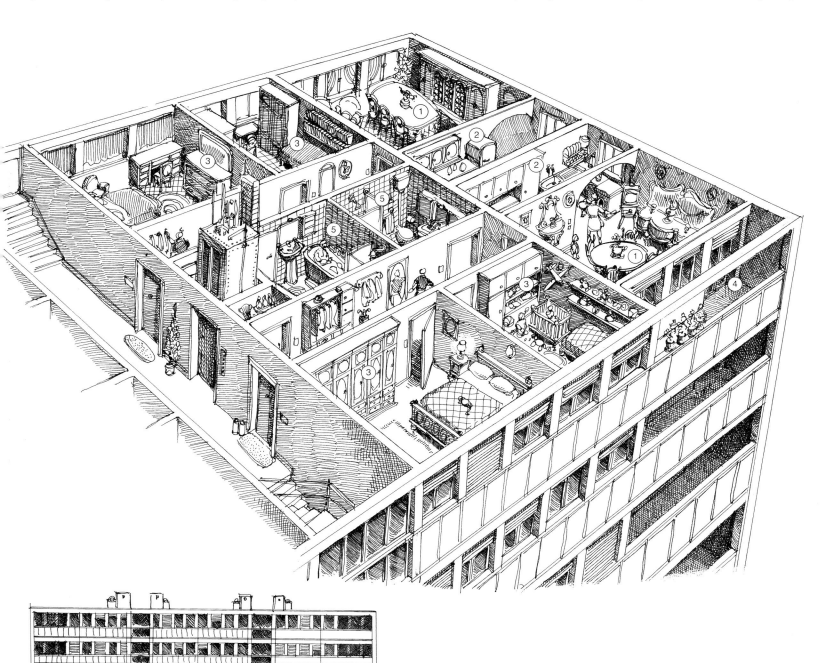

LIFE IN A 100-SQ. METRE SPACE

By comparison to life in a house in times gone by, life in a flat was incredibly cramped. Most flats were no larger than 100 square metres. They were, however, comfortable and well equipped; there was electricity, gas, a telephone, and many household gadgets that took the labour out of housework and gave people more free time.

1. Living room
2. Kitchen
3. Bedrooms
4. Balcony
5. Bathroom
6. Plan of the two flats that made up each floor of the block

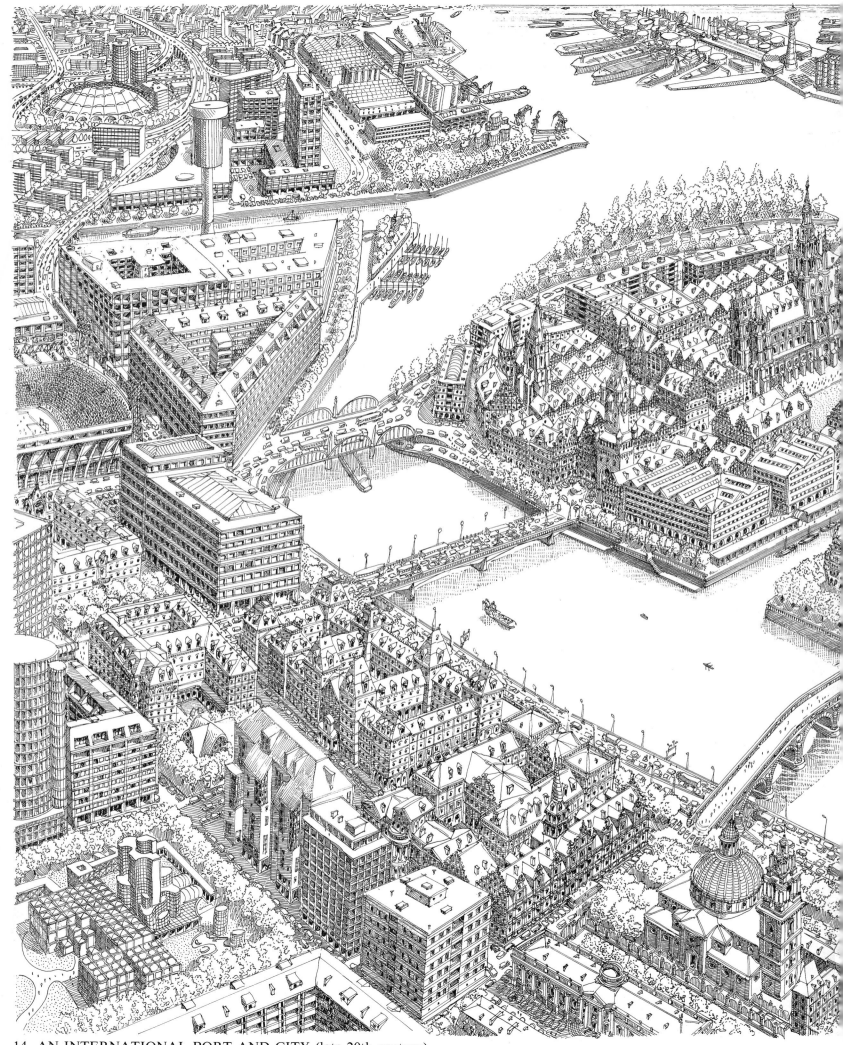

14. AN INTERNATIONAL PORT AND CITY (late 20th century)

14. AN INTERNATIONAL PORT AND CITY
(LATE 20TH CENTURY)

A downturn in the economy of the 1970s and '80s had contributed to the change in living conditions in Lebek. The industrial city that had grown up during the 19th century now became less industrial and more of an administrative centre. Light industry moved further out, or transferred operations to other countries where labour was cheaper, and the offices of many national companies moved in to take its place. Lebek had now become a major European city, and a centre of international standing.

By the end of the 20th century, Lebek, although extremely large, had achieved a feeling of harmony and order, and life in the city was not unpleasant.

The apparent downturn in the economy towards the end of the 20th century did not affect Lebek's overseas trade, on which the city had depended throughout its history. The port evolved into one of the most modern and well-equipped in northern Europe.

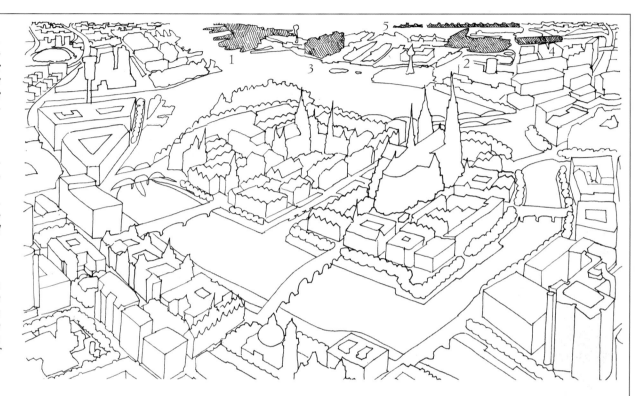

1. Oil and petrol docks
Loading and unloading oil, petrol and diesel was highly automated. The bureaucratic process began almost as soon as the ship entered harbour. The freight was unloaded immediately on docking.

2. Container docks
On account of its many advantages, containerization was widely used in the late 20th century. These enormous boxes were lifted by special cranes. Specially designed container ships carried the cargo.

3. Warehouses and silos
The port was equipped with different kinds of warehouses specially designed for storing different sorts of goods. The great silos, which stood out on the skyline, held various types of grain, such as wheat and soya.

4. Access to the port
Trains reached the port along a special network of railway lines. Container lorries used roads that serviced the port.

5. Dykes and coastal defences
Enormous sea defences with gates that could be closed whenever danger threatened were built along the coast. Lowlands reclaimed from the sea were now protected forever against fierce coastal storms.

1. **Container ship**
2. **Crane for loading and unloading containers**
3. **Fork lift truck**
4. **Storage area for containers**
5. **Container lorries**
6. **Railway for container wagons**

CONTAINER SHIPPING
Metal containers were ideal for transporting all kinds of goods quickly and safely. Customs officers checked their contents in the country of origin or when they were unloaded. The cargo meanwhile travelled safely inside the containers, the size of which was standardized so that container ships, lorries and freight trains could handle them more easily. It was simple and cheap to load and unload the containers.

Thanks to the European Community, Europe as a whole had also become more closely-knit economically, and because of this the port of Lebek became even more important. A steady stream of ships from all over the world called to unload cargoes destined for Europe. Containers were unloaded on to well-equipped, well-organized quays, and handling charges paid. Then, using the efficient network of roads and railways, goods could be speedily delivered to any country in Europe.

At this time, oil was the fuel on which the economies of western Europe depended, and supertankers brought crude oil from distant countries to the port. Large storage tanks were built to hold the oil and store it ready for distribution.

The dock complex grew ever larger as quays, dockyards and storage facilities were built out into the sea. At the same time, the task of reclaiming land and protecting it from the ravages of the sea continued. Using modern technology, great dykes were built against the tides. A system of locks ensured that the waters were kept under control, and to protect and conserve wildlife habitats.

At the end of the 20th century, Lebek, which had literally grown out of the sea, once again looked overseas for its future prosperity.

SEA WALLS

Strong sea walls linking artificial islands and areas of dry land were built to protect the coastline and the low-lying lands that had been reclaimed from the sea. This was because storms frequently caused disastrous flooding. Roads ran along the top of the sea walls. Barriers that could be opened and closed when necessary, allowed water to flow in during calm weather: salty water was essential for the shellfish farms as well as for the plants and animals of the estuary. During stormy weather, the barriers prevented the heaving waters from flooding the land.

Under the sea walls the sea-bed was compressed and a bedding of plastic, sand, gravel, pebbles and wire laid down to make the ground firm. Then concrete pylons, especially treated to withstand the force of the sea, were lowered into the water and supported at the base with stone blocks.

1. **Compressing the sea-bed**
2. **Laying the plastic, sand, gravel, pebble and wire bedding**
3. **Positioning the pylon's foundation**
4. **Building up the pylon**
5. **Protecting the base of the pylon**
6. **Pylons**
7. **Barriers**

GLOSSARY

Allegiance Loyalty.

Alum A chemical compound containing aluminium.

Apse The curved end of a church, behind the main altar or containing it.

Aqueduct A pipe or canal used to carry water over a long distance.

Archimedean screw A device to raise water by means of a rotating spiral cylinder.

Arsenal A store of arms and military equipment.

Barbarians Brutal and uncivilized people.

Baroque A style of art and architecture characterized by ornate decoration. It was popular from the late 16th to early 18th centuries.

Bridgehead A fortified position at the end of a bridge.

Buttresses Stone constructions built to support a wall.

Carding machines Machines for processing wool or cotton fibres for spinning.

Caulkers People who packed the gaps between the planks of a ship's hull with waterproof material to prevent leaks.

Coffer dam A watertight structure that encloses an area under water.

Desalinated water Water that has had the salt removed from it.

Draught The depth of a loaded vessel in the water.

Entrepreneur The owner of a business enterprise, who by taking risks and iniative, attempts to make profits.

Façade The face or main front of a building.

Flemish Relating to Flemings, inhabitants of Flanders (part of present-day Belgium).

Foundry A place where metal castings are produced.

Friars Members of a religious order.

Gables The triangular upper part of a wall between the sloping ends of a roof.

Germanic Relating to the peoples of northern Europe.

Ghettoes Densely populated slum areas of a city.

Gothic A style of architecture in western Europe used from the 12th to 16th centuries, characterized by ribbed vaulted ceilings, narrow pointed arches and flying buttresses.

Graeco-Roman Relating to Ancient Greek and Roman influences.

Hanseatic League A commercial association of towns, formed in the mid-14th century in North Germany, to protect and control trade.

Hawser A large heavy rope.

Hinterland Land lying behind the coast.

Hydroelectric power Electric power driven by the force of falling water.

Imperial Relating to an empire, emperor or empress.

Incendiary bombs Bombs that are designed to cause fires.

Internal combustion engine A heat engine such as a petrol or gas engine.

Lock A section of a canal, river or dock that can be closed off to control the water level for the raising and lowering of vessels.

Megalith A stone of great size, forming part of an historic monument.

Megalithic culture The traditions of the people who moved the megaliths in order to build temples.

Menhir A standing stone, often carved, dating from about 3000 BC.

Migrations The movement of people from one country to another.

Nave The central space in a church.

Neo-classical A style of architecture of the late 18th and early 19th centuries, imitating the styles of Ancient Greece and Rome.

Picardy A region in northern France.

Piracy Robbery on the seas.

Ramparts Fortified walls built for defence.

Revenue Income from taxation.

Ridge roof A roof with sloping sides.

Romanesque A style of architecture used in western and southern Europe from the 9th to 12th century, characterized by massive wall construction and rounded arches.

Scuttled When a vessel has been deliberatedly made to sink.

Shipwrights Workers skilled in building ships.

Silo A tall building for storing grain.

Sluice gates Gates that control the flow of water through a channel.

Spinning jenny An early type of spinning frame.

Spooling machine A machine for winding thread.

Stocks A frame used to support a boat while under construction.

Stonemasons People skilled in preparing stone for building.

Town planning The planning of the construction and social development of a town.

Transept Wing of a cruciform church, at right angles to the nave.

United Provinces A Dutch republic formed by the union of seven northern provinces of the Netherlands from 1581 to 1795.

FURTHER READING

Gibson, Michael *The Vikings* (Wayland, 2nd impression 1987)

Hope, Robert *Cities* (Macdonald, 1984)

Neal, Philip *The Urban Scene* (Dryad Press, 1987)

Ross, Stuart *Spotlight on Medieval Europe* (Wayland, 1985)

INDEX